OUR MOTHER TONGUE

ANSWER KEY

Our Mother Tongue
Answer Key

Nancy Wilson

canonpress
Moscow, Idaho

Published by Canon Press
P.O. Box 8729, Moscow, ID 83843
800–488–2034 | www.canonpress.com

Nancy Wilson, *Our Mother Tongue Answer Key*
Copyright ©2004 by Nancy Wilson

Cover design by Paige Atwood.
Interior design by Jared Miller.
ISBN-13: 978-1-59128-016-3
ISBN-10: 1-59128-016-8

10 11 12 13 14 15 16 17 18 19 20   15 14 13 12 11 10 9 8 7

Contents

Unit 1: The Eight Classes of Words

Lesson 1: Nouns

Exercise B

1. crack, rocks, grains, substance, recesses
2. spring, summer, tails, wind, tails, things, will, direction, wind
3. leaves, deal, noise, wind
4. time, tree, wind, tail, creature, appendage, summer-time, peacock, expanse, plumage

Lesson 2: Verbs

Exercise D

1. will become
2. seems
3. will be
4. is
5. must be

Review Exercise A

1. brevity, soul, wit; linking verb: is.
2. boys, tickets, game; verb: were (helping verb) selling.
3. cars, clouds, dust; verbs: raced, raised.
4. woods, colors, autumn; verbs: walked, enjoyed.
5. paint, sides, barn; verbs: was (helping) peeling.

Review Exercise B

Nouns:

1. houses, advantage, coachmen, chairmen, porters, boys, London (proper), portion.
2. marks, ignorant, shops, signs, aspect, streets.
3. evening, difficulty, danger, walking,* London (proper), windows, pails, regard.
4. falls, bruises, bones, occurrence, year, reign, Charles the Second (proper), streets, darkness.
5. thieves, robbers, trades, impunity, citizens, class, ruffians.
6. amusement, gentlemen, night, town, windows, sedans, men, caresses, women.

* *Walking*, though it can be a verb, is used here to name an activity.

Verbs:

1. were numbered, have been, could read.
2. was, (to use*), could understand.,were distinguished, gave.
3. closed, became, were opened, were emptied, were passing.
4. were, were left.
5. plied, were.
6. was, (to swagger*), breaking, upsetting, beating, offering.

LESSON 3: ADJECTIVES

EXERCISE B

1. A, the, blank
2. An, a, a

3. The
4. Blank, a

EXERCISE E

1. quiet, old: town; prettiest: place.
2. long, wide: streets; gigantic, American (proper adjective): elms; drooping: branches; graceful: arches.
3. small, gay: flower-gardens; massive: chimney-stacks; protruding: eaves.
4. beautiful: river; tiny: islands.

LESSON 4: ADVERBS

EXERCISE B

Adjectives: The, merry, little, the, tall
Nouns: man, branch, tree
Verbs: sang
Adverbs: cheerily, very

REVIEW EXERCISE A

Abbreviations for *noun, verb, adjective,* and *adverb* will follow each word in parentheses.

1. It was(v) a brilliant (adj) moonlit (adj) night (n), but extremely (adv) cold (adj); our (adj) chaise (n) whirled (v) rapidly (adv) over the frozen (adj) ground (n); the noisy

---

* A verb with *to* in front of it is an *infinitive,* and not a verb. Infinitives will be treated in the unit on verbals. In sentence 2, the infinitive *to use* modifies *necessary* as an adverb. In sentence 6, the infinitive *to swagger* is an adjective modifying *amusement.*

(adj) postboy (n) smacked (v) his (adj) long (adj) whip (n) incessantly (adv), and a part (n) of the time (n) his (adj) horses (n) galloped (v).

2. "He knows (v) he is going (v) home,"(adv) said (v) my (adj) companion (n), "and is (v) eager (adj) for some of the merriment (n) and good (adj) cheer (n) of the servants' (adj) hall (n).

3. My (adj) father (n) is (v) a gentleman (n) of the old (adj) school (n), and takes (v) pride (n) in old (adj) English (proper adj) hospitality."(n)

4. On our (adj) arrival (n), the squire (n) came (v) out (adv) and received (v) us. He was (v) a fine (adj) , healthy-looking (adj) old (adj) gentleman (n), with silver (adj) hair. (n)

5. As the evening (n) was (v) far (adv) advanced (adj), the squire (n) quickly (adv) ushered (v) us into the company (n), which was assembled (v) in a large (adj), old-fashioned (adj) hall. (n)

LESSON 5: THE PRONOUN

EXERCISE A

1. Jan bought *herself* a set of dishes.
2. *She* later realized that *she* did not need *them* as much as *her* sister Kate did.
3. So *she* gave *them* to *her*.
4. Kate was pleased that Jan had been so generous to *her*.

EXERCISE B

The personal pronouns and possessive pronouns are in italics. The possessive pronouns are followed with an (a) for adjective.

1. Then the chief butler spoke to Pharaoh, saying: "*I* remember *my* (a) faults this day.
2. When Pharaoh was angry with *his* (a) servants, and put *me* in custody in the house of the captain of the guard, both *me* and the chief baker, *we* each had a dream in one night, *he* and *I*.
3. Each of *us* dreamed according to the interpretation of *his* (a) own dream.
4. Now there was a young Hebrew man with *us* there, a servant of the captain of the guard.
5. And *we* told *him*, and *he* interpreted *our* (a) dreams for *us*; to each man *he* interpreted according to *his* (a) own dream.
6. And *it* came to pass, just as *he* interpreted for *us*, so *it* happened.
7. *He* restored *me* to *my* (a) office, and *he* hanged *him*."
8. Then Pharaoh sent and called Joseph, and *they* brought *him* quickly out of the dungeon; and *he* shaved, changed *his* (a) clothing, and came to Pharaoh.

9. And Pharaoh said to Joseph, "*I* have had a dream, and there is no one who can interpret *it.*
10. But *I* have heard *it* said of *you* that *you* can understand a dream, to interpret *it.*"

LESSON 6: THE PREPOSITION
EXERCISE A
The prepositions are italicized below. The objects are underlined.
1. Did you find your homework *in* the <u>car</u>?
2. *After* <u>dinner</u> they went *to* the <u>theater</u>.
3. The child sat *on* her <u>lap</u> *until* <u>bedtime</u>.
4. *Besides* her <u>mother</u>, no one else came *to* the <u>recital</u>.
5. We've had no rain *since* <u>September</u>.
6. Step *into* the <u>bus</u> quickly.
7. *Without* her <u>textbook</u>, she is lost *in* science <u>class</u>.
8. Go *past* the gas <u>station</u> and turn right *on* <u>Hayes Street</u>.
9. *During* <u>dinner</u> we had three phone calls *from* <u>salesmen</u>.
10. *Throughout* the <u>winter</u> we saw flocks *of* <u>geese</u> flying *over* our <u>house</u>.

REVIEW EXERCISE
All the nouns (n), pronouns (p), verbs (v), adjectives (adj), adverbs (adv), and prepositions (prep) are identified with abbreviations following each.

Now the eyes (n) of (prep) Israel (n) were (v) dim (adj) with (prep) age (n), so that he (p) could (v) not (adv) see (v). Then (adv) Joseph (n) brought (v) them (p) near (prep) him (p), and he (p) kissed (v) them (p) and embraced (v) them (p). So Joseph (n) brought (v) them (p) from (prep) beside (prep) his (adj) knees (n), and he (p) bowed (v) down (adv) with (prep) his (adj) face (n) to (prep) the earth (n). And Joseph (n) took (v) them (p) both, Ephraim (n) with (prep) his (adj) right (adj) hand (n) toward (prep) Israel's (adj) left (adj) hand (n), and Manasseh (n) with (prep) his (adj) left (adj) hand (n) toward (prep) Israel's (adj) right (adj) hand (n), and brought (v) them (p) near (prep) him (p).

LESSON 7: THE CONJUNCTION
EXERCISE C
The conjunctions are in italics and identified as coordinating (cd) or correlative (co).
1. *Both* animals *and* plants live and grow. (co)
2. The mother wept, *for* her son was dead. (cd)

3. Thomas sat down, *but* his little sister ran away. (cd)

4. All seek happiness, *yet* not all find it. (cd)

5. *Neither* soldiers *nor* sailors were available to fight. (co)

6. *Whether* you go *or* not does not concern me. (co)

7. They may be slow, *but* they are sure. (cd)

8. *Either* finish your supper *or* excuse yourself from the table. (co)

9. He is *not only* ill, *but* he is *also* weak. (co)

10. Stan *as well as* Dave passed the test. (cd)

Lesson 8: The Interjection

Exercise A

The interjections in the following sentences are italicized.

1. *Quiet!* You should not be talking.

2. *Yikes!* I broke my ankle!

3. *Oh!* I didn't know it was you.

4. *Good heavens!* What a mess you've made.

5. *Wow!* What a beautiful day!

6. *Ouch!* I cut my finger.

Lesson 9: Review

Exercise A

1. The (adj) Lord (n) is (v) my (adj) shepherd (n); I (p) shall (v) not (adv) want (v).

2. He (p) makes (v) me (p) (to) lie (v) down (adv) in (prep) green (adj) pastures (n).

3. He (p) leads (v) me (p) beside (prep) the (adj) still (adj) waters (n).

4. He (p) restores (v) my (adj) soul (n).

5. He (p) leads (v) me (p) in (prep) the (adj) paths (n) of (prep) righteousness (n) for (prep) His (adj) name's (adj) sake (n).

Exercise D

Note: In sentence 11, *where* is an adverb introducing an adjective clause; *though* in sentence 13 and *because* in 14 are both subordinating conjunctions. These are marked with an asterisk and are covered later in the book.

1. James (n) writes (v) very (adv) well (adv).

2. The (adj) Apostles (n) preached (v) the (adj) gospel (n).

3. Jesus Christ (n) was (v) rich (adj), yet (con) He (p) became (v) poor (adj).

4. The (adj) Scriptures (n) teach (v) love (n) to (prep) God (n) and (con) man (n).

5. Good (adj) and (con) wise (adj) men (n) make (v) valuable (adj) friends (n).

6. A (adj) wise (adj) son (n) hears (v) the (adj) instructions (n) of (prep) a (adj) father (n).

7. Envy (n) and (con) anger (n) cause (v) great (adj) pain (n), and (con) they (p) shorten (v) life (n).

8. Anger (n) rests (v) in (prep) the (adj) bosom (n) of (prep) wicked (adj) men (n).

9. A (adj) good (adj) man (n) dismisses (v) all (adj) unkind (adj) feelings (n).

10. Death (n) to (prep) good (adj) men (n) is (v) the (adj) gate (n) of (prep) Heaven (n).

11. A (adj) hospital (n) is (v) a (adj) place (n) where (* adv) sick (adj) persons (n) are (v) received (v).

12. A (adj) thoughtful (adj) mind (n) will (v) find (v) instruction (n) in (prep) all (adj) things (n).

13. God (n) has (v) shown (v) love (n) to (prep) man (n), though (*) man (n) returns (v) it (p) not (adv).

14. We (p) defer (v) repentance (n) to (prep) some (adj) future (adj) time (n), because (*) we (p) love (v) sin (n).

15. In (prep) books (n) we (p) find (v) much (adj) valuable (adj) instruction (n).

Unit Two: The Sentence

Lesson 10: Kinds of Sentences

Exercise B

1. The farmers are harvesting the wheat. (Declarative)
2. Tell me what you are thinking. (Imperative)
3. Where are you going after class? (Interrogative)
4. How dark the sky is! (Exclamatory)
5. Call my brother back. (Imperative, and with an exclamation point, also Exclamatory)
6. My locker is very full of books. (Declarative)
7. His birthday is next month. (Declarative)
8. What is the answer to question number four? (Interrogative)
9. Be quiet. (Imperative, and with an exclamation point, also Exclamatory)
10. What a day I've had! (Exclamatory)

Exercise C

1. The bonfire burned brightly.
   Did the bonfire burn brightly?
   Let the bonfire burn brightly.
   How brightly the bonfire burns!
2. The morning flew by.
   Did the morning fly by?
   Let the morning fly by.
   How the morning flew by!
3. The wind blew fiercely.
   Did the wind blow fiercely?
   Let the wind blow fiercely.
   How fiercely the wind blows!
4. The students read eagerly.
   Do the students read eagerly?
   Let the students read eagerly.
   How eagerly the students read!
5. The wedding was lovely.
   Was the wedding lovely?

Let it be a lovely wedding.
What a lovely wedding!

LESSON 11: THE SUBJECT

EXERCISE A

In the following exercises the subjects are italicized.

1. A *band* was playing in the park.
2. The football *game* was canceled.
3. *She* showed me her photographs.
4. *We* rode home.
5. The *sunset* was glorious.

EXERCISE B

1. *Dogs* and *cats* are America's favorite pets.
2. The *students* and *parents* gathered for school orientation.
3. My *shelf* is full of my favorite books.
4. *Robinson Crusoe* and *Pilgrim's Progress* are among them.
5. *Ketchup, mayonnaise,* and *mustard* were served with the hamburgers.

EXERCISE C

The subjects in the sentences below are italicized.

1. At the doorstep on summer evenings sat the little stray *dog*.
2. A *noun* or a *pronoun* can be used as a subject.
3. *Adjectives* and *adverbs* are called modifiers.
4. Up into the clouds went the *balloon* and *string*.
5. What bright blue eyes *she* has!
6. In the dark shade of the forest stands an old *house* and a weather-beaten *barn*.
7. Are *Sue* and *David* coming to dinner tonight?
8. Three little *girls* were giggling in the corner.
9. *Sam* and *Judy* will be here soon.
10. *Latin* and *literature* are his favorite classes this year.

LESSON 12: THE PREDICATE
EXERCISE C

1. *Dogs growl.*

Dogs	growl

2. *Boys are watching.*

Boys	are watching

3. *Teams are competing.*

Teams	are competing

4. *Houses have been built.*

Houses	have been built

5. *I am studying.*

I	am studying

EXERCISE D

1. *Poplars and willows were planted.*

Poplars

willows | and | were planted

3. *Mom and Dad are walking and jogging.*

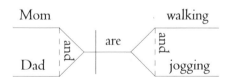

2. *Dave and Jill are touring and traveling.*

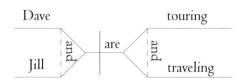

LESSON 13: THE SUBJECT MODIFIED BY AN ADJECTIVE

EXERCISE B

1. She has an old, old necklace that was her grandmother's.

2. Sam wrote a clear, precise, intelligent essay that won him the prize.

3. His classmates viewed him as reserved and proud, ambitious and haughty.

4. The tired, drooping, hungry preschoolers toddled off the bus.

5. He drove a shiny, new, bright red pickup in the parade.

EXERCISE C

1. *His old family Bible was treasured.*

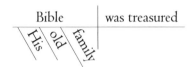

2. *Several favorite passages were underlined.*

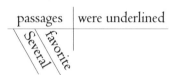

3. *All the important family dates were recorded.*

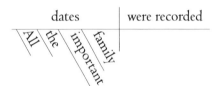

4. *The black leather cover was cracking.*

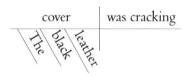

LESSON 14: THE SUBJECT MODIFIED BY A POSSESSIVE PRO-NOUN

EXERCISE A

1. Child's, prince's, baby's, teacher's, uncle's.

2. Father's, cat's, John's, dog's, mercy's.

3. Bible's, verse's, painter's, sister's, house's.

4. Charles's, Jesus', princess's, bridge's, foxes'.

5. Williamses', Xerxes', Davis's, geese's.

LESSON 15: THE SUBJECT MODIFIED BY AN APPOSITIVE

EXERCISE A

The appositives and appositive phrases are italicized in the sentences below.

1. David, *the psalmist,* was a man after God's own heart.
2. Our faithful dog, *a golden retriever,* guards the house.
3. My father, *a veteran of World War II,* has several medals for heroism.
4. *A fine student and leader,* Sam will go places.
5. *My daughter* Sarah is my best friend.

EXERCISE B

1. Mr. Gibbs, the new science teacher, will speak at the assembly today.
2. The new library, a beautiful brick building, will be quite an asset to the community.
3. The boys' piano teacher, Mrs. Williams, will come for supper tonight.
4. Latin, a language considered dead by many people, is the source of over half of English vocabulary.
5. Jim Miller, the new boy on the team, came from Texas.

EXERCISE C

1. *My favorite book,* Pride and Prejudice, *has been reviewed.*

| book   (*Pride and Prejudice*) | has been reviewed |

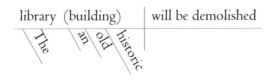

3. *Her puppy, a chocolate lab, is barking.*

| puppy   (lab) | is barking |

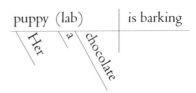

2. *The library, an old historic building, will be demolished.*

| library   (building) | will be demolished |

LESSON 16: THE SUBJECT MODIFIED BY AN ADJECTIVE PHRASE

EXERCISE A

Example adjective phrases are given below.

1. The storm blew down a barn *in the neighborhood.*

2. A table *of oak* fills the dining room.

3. Women *of virtue* are pleasing to God.

4. We listened to a speech *about history.*

5. She is a woman *with sense.*

EXERCISE B

The adjective phrases are italicized and the nouns they modify are underlined.

1. A <u>house</u> *of stone* is not uncommon in England.

2. A <u>tourist</u> *from Australia* visited us last week.

3. <u>Roads</u> *in the country* are muddy in the spring.

4. <u>Grapes</u> *from California* make fine wine.

5. The <u>car</u> *with the broken headlight* is mine.

EXERCISE D

1. *The princess from a faraway land was kidnapped.*   2. *A prince on a white stallion arrived.*

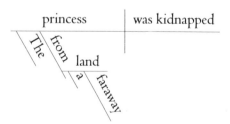
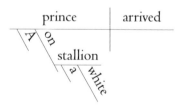

3. *His kind offer of rescue was accepted.*

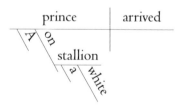

Lesson 17: The Subject Modified By An Adjective Clause

Exercise A

The adjective clause is in italics, the noun modified is underlined, and the relative pronoun is bold.

1. <u>He</u> **who** *heeds the word wisely* will find good.
2. There is a <u>way</u> **that** *seems right to a man*, but its end is the way of death.
3. <u>He</u> **who** *has knowledge* spares his words, and a man of understanding is of a calm spirit.
4. Better is the <u>poor</u> **who** *walks in his integrity* than <u>one</u> **who** *is perverse in his lips*, and is a fool.
5. <u>Blows</u> **that** *hurt* cleanse away evil.

Exercise C

The adjective clauses are italicized.

1. This is the room *where we will have the reception.*
2. Here is the book *I bought.*
3. That is the reason *why I am late.*
4. May is the month *when he will graduate.*
5. Now is the time *when we should go.*

Exercise D

1. *The package that is in the hall is moving.*

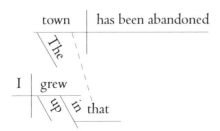

2. *The vase which fell shattered.*

3. *The town that I grew up in has been abandoned.*

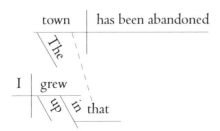

4. *The boy who laughed was corrected.*

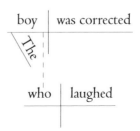

LESSON 18: THE PREDICATE MODIFIED BY AN ADVERB

EXERCISE A

1. I *politely* but *firmly* told the salesman I was *not* interested.
2. He *resolutely* continued with his sales pitch.
3. I *calmly* told my daughter the news.
4. He said he would call *tomorrow*, but he *never* did.
5. She is climbing *down now*.

EXERCISE B

1. *The small child cried angrily.*

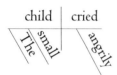

2. *The bright yellow daffodils were blooming cheerily.*

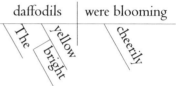

3. *Several small boys were playing noisily.*

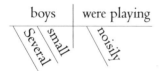

4. *The rustic cabin was surprisingly abandoned.*

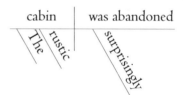

5. *Today he suddenly left.*

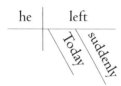

LESSON 19: THE PREDICATE MODIFIED BY AN ADVERB PHRASE

EXERCISE A

The adverb phrases are italicized in the sentences below.

1. A basket of goodies sat *by the door*.
2. *From the window* of the train we saw an old brick schoolhouse.

3. Man shall not live *by bread* alone.

4. She arrived *at London in the morning* and stayed *for two days.*

5. We waited *for him for several minutes,* but we left *in a hurry.*

6. The dog jumped *over the fence in pursuit* of the cat.

7. Wait *on the Lord.*

8. The youngster confided *in his mother about his hopes* for a Christmas gift.

9. The track team ran *around the track in the pouring rain.*

10. *From the roof* we can see *beyond the mountains.*

EXERCISE B

1. *The streets in Moscow are covered with snow.*

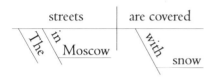

2. *A toddler with his mother's purse wandered out the door and into the yard.*

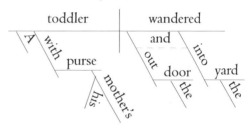

3. *In early spring many tulips bloom in the park on the campus.*

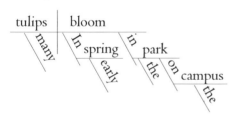

4. *They shopped for several hours at the mall.*

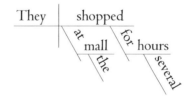

5. *Thousands of stars appeared in the sky.*

LESSON 20: THE PREDICATE MODIFIED BY AN ADVERB CLAUSE

EXERCISE A

The adverb clauses are in italics, and the subordinate conjunctions are underlined.

1. Mom sewed on my dress *while I watched the little ones.*
2. The sky looked *as if it might rain any minute.*
3. *Wherever I walked in the garden,* I only saw more splendid sights.
4. Susan brought Sam home *so that we could meet him.*
5. She set the vase of flowers *where we all could see it.*
6. *When you are ready for us,* call us.
7. *After she had washed the crystal,* she gently set it in the hutch.
8. She polished the silver *because it was tarnished quite badly.*
9. *As soon as he finished his test,* he smiled with relief.
10. He ran with the ball *as though he were going for a touchdown.*

EXERCISE C

1. *David looks as though he already knew.*

2. *We will go if the team wins.*

3. *You should read whenever you can.*

4. *Unless he arrives soon, the game will be canceled.*

5. *As soon as you finish, I will begin.*

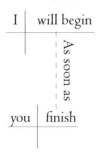

LESSON 21: THE PREDICATE WITH A DIRECT OBJECT

EXERCISE A

The direct objects in the sentences below are in italics.

1. Ben kicked the *ball* across the field for a goal.
2. You hit the *nail* on the head!
3. He pushed the *sofa* to the den.
4. She lost her *purse.*
5. Mom wrote a *check* for their trip.
6. He's reading <u>*A Tale of Two Cities*</u> for literature class.
7. She bought six new *trees* for the yard.
8. The band played several *songs* from the forties.
9. I could not read the *sign* in the dark.
10. He loaded the *luggage* into the trunk of the car.

EXERCISE B

1. *The church choir sang Christmas carols at the concert.*

2. *She pasted a stamp on the envelope.*

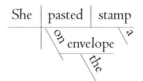

3. *The child licked the lollipop joyously.*

4. *He opened the letter nervously.*

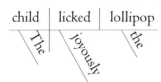

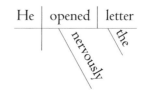

5. *We all enjoy football games at outdoor stadiums.*

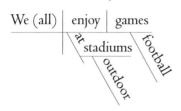

6. *She reached the meeting on time.*

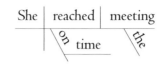

7. *They attended their aunt's funeral in June.*

8. *The committee sent their findings.*

9. *The new teacher wrote her name on the board.*

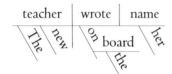

10. *I heard the birds this morning.*

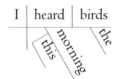

LESSON 22: THE PREDICATE WITH AN INDIRECT OBJECT

EXERCISE A

The indirect objects are underlined; the direct objects are in italics.

1. The company gave the <u>school</u> a large *grant* for computers.
2. The instructor handed the <u>students</u> a long reading *list.*
3. You promised <u>me</u> your cookie *recipe.*
4. Give <u>Charles</u> my *greeting.*
5. She sang the <u>baby</u> a *lullaby.*
6. Mother baked the <u>senior class</u> a *cake* for their graduation party.
7. My sister made <u>me</u> a velvet *dress.*
8. The babysitter read the <u>children</u> a *story.*
9. I ordered <u>myself</u> a new *desk.*
10. We poured <u>Mother</u> some *tea.*

EXERCISE B

1. *The baby gave me a smile.*

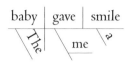

2. *Mom sent the college a letter of recommendation.*

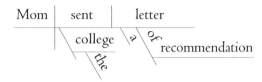

3. *He gave the class a long lecture.*

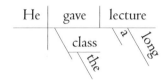

4. *My host ordered me a cocktail.*

5. *The hostess handed me a napkin.*

LESSON 23: THE PREDICATE WITH A PREDICATE NOMINATIVE

EXERCISE A

The predicate nominatives in the sentences below are in italics.

1. Raphael was an *artist*.
2. The whale is the largest *mammal*.
3. Tadpoles become *frogs*.
4. Faithfulness is a *virtue*.
5. The church is the *bride* of Christ.
6. The boy was a *dunce*.
7. Lewis and Clark were famous *explorers*.
8. Jeremy is a fine *athlete*.
9. The moon is not a *star*.
10. The boy is my *nephew*.

EXERCISE C

The predicate nominatives in these sentences are in italics.

1. Children are a *heritage* from the Lord.
2. The fruit of the womb is His *reward.*
3. Your children are olive *plants* around your table.
4. Your wife shall be a fruitful *vine.*
5. My soul is a weaned *child* within me.
6. The idols of the nations are *silver* and *gold.*
7. Their tongues are *serpents* full of poison.
8. You are my *refuge,* O Lord.
9. You are my *portion* in the land of the living.
10. The Lord is the *One* who gives salvation to kings.

EXERCISE D

1. *My favorite herb is rosemary.*

herb | is \ rosemary
My \ favorite

2. *Susie's brother is an attorney.*

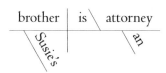

3. *My favorite sport is basketball.*

sport | is \ basketball
My \ favorite

4. *This is our new teacher.*

This | is \ teacher
our \ new

5. *That was her best race.*

That | was \ race
her \ best

LESSON 24: THE PREDICATE WITH A PREDICATE ADJECTIVE

EXERCISE A

The predicate adjectives in the sentences below are in italics.

1. He is *happy* who has the God of Jacob for his help.
2. The Lord is *righteous*.
3. Lord, my heart is not *haughty*; my eyes are not *lofty*.
4. The Lord is *good* to all.
5. Your tabernacle is *lovely*, O Lord of Hosts!
6. That fragrance smells *sweet*.
7. Do not be *unwise*.
8. He is *worthy* of the honor.
9. The owl looks *wise*.
10. The children seemed *happy*.

Exercise C

1. *She was tired and cranky.*

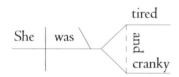

2. *The field was golden with ripe wheat.*

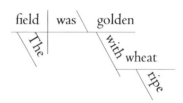

3. *The air smells fresh and clean.*

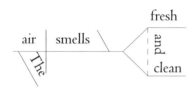

4. *The young man seemed honest and upright.*

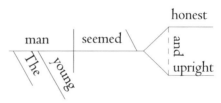

5. *The puppy was soft and cuddly.*

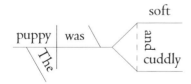

6. *This plum tastes terrible.*

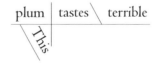

7. *The stars are brilliant tonight.*

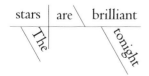

8. *You are wrong.*

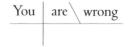

9. *The class was well-behaved today.*

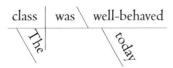

10. *The snow became slushy quickly.*

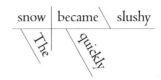

LESSON 25: THE NOUN CLAUSE

EXERCISE A

The noun clauses in the following sentences are in italics. They are identified in parentheses as subject, direct object, object of the preposition, predicate nominative, or appositive in the sentence.

1. I know *what you want.* (D. O.)
2. The fact *that the roof leaks* is the reason for the low price. (App.)
3. *Whether it rains or snows* never affects her travel plans. (Subj.)
4. *Whoever applies for the job* will be considered. (Subj.)
5. The teacher said *that our tests were graded.* (D. O.)
6. *Why you bought tickets to Alaska* is beyond me. (Subj.)
7. The lawn will be watered by *whoever housesits for us.* (Obj. Prep.)
8. The reason for the notice is *that he hasn't paid his bill.* (Pred. Nom.)
9. I must write Mother about *how she sang.* (Obj. Prep.)
10. She told me *that she had already called you.* (D. O.)

EXERCISE B

In the following sentences noun, adjective, and adverb clauses are italicized and identified.

1. *Whenever I travel* (adverb), I pack only *what I absolutely need.* (noun)
2. No one knows *whether he is going to school in the fall.* (noun)
3. Experienced travelers, *who must travel frequently for their jobs* (adj.), usually know *where the best deals are.* (noun)
4. The flight *that we took from San Francisco* (adj.) was very crowded.
5. *Because the flight was so long* (adv.), I felt very groggy *when we arrived.* (adv.)
6. The meal *that they served* (adj.) wasn't bad.
7. *That we made it safely home* (noun) was my chief desire.
8. I don't know *how long I slept.* (noun)
9. One of the complaints about the food was *that it was cold.* (noun)
10. *When the wind blows at our house* (adv.), the windows shake.

Exercise C

1. *I heard that you have lost your watch.*

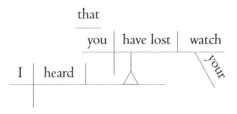

2. *I know they will do what is right.*

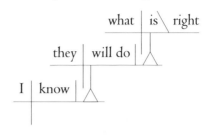

3. *That they lost the first two games did not discourage them.*

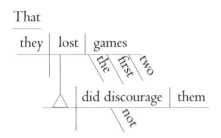

4. *I bet his plane will be late.*

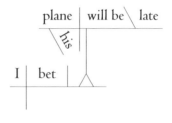

5. *The truth is that I am exhausted.*

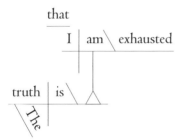

6. *I will give you whatever is fair.*

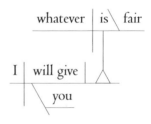

7. *What his plans are will be a surprise.*

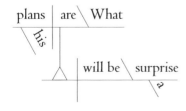

8. *That some pages are missing is a problem with the book.*

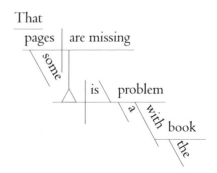

9. *Invite whomever you want.*

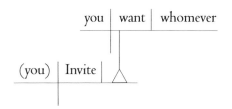

10. *The buildings will be painted by whomever he hires for the summer.*

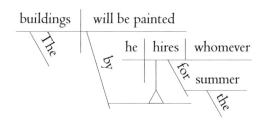

Lesson 26: Sentence Structure

Exercise A

The following sentences are identified as simple (s), compound (cd), complex (cx), or compound-complex (cd-cx).

1. A righteous man who falters before the wicked is like a murky spring and a polluted well (Prov. 25:26). Cx
2. He who gives a right answer kisses the lips (Prov. 24:26). Cx
3. He who covers his sin will not prosper (Prov. 28:13a). Cx
4. Do not forsake your own friend or your father's friend, nor go to your brother's house in the day of your calamity (Prov. 27:10a). S
5. Whoever walks blamelessly will be saved, but he who is perverse in his ways will fall at once (Prov. 28:18). Cd-cx

Exercise B

1. *Who can find a virtuous wife?*

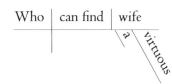

2. *The heart of her husband safely trusts her, so he will have no lack of gain.*

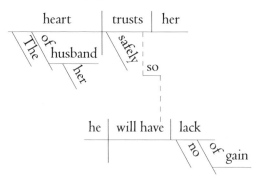

3. *She seeks wool and flax, and willingly works with her hands.*

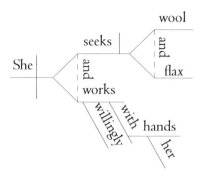

4. *She also rises while it is yet night, and provides food for her household and a portion for her maidservants.*

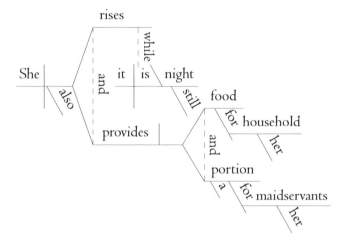

5. *Her husband is known in the gates when he sits among the elders of the land.*

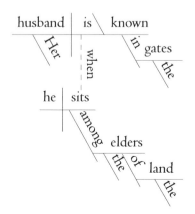

LESSON 27: REVIEW

EXERCISE A: MODIFYING THE SUBJECT

Suggestions for adjectives (or possessive nouns) are in parentheses.

1. The (Mom's, old) swing gently rocked in the wind.
2. My (new) car needs repairs.
3. The (big, gray) clouds covered the mountain.

Examples in parentheses.

1. The swing (on the porch) gently rocked in the wind.
2. My car (from my grandma) needs repairs.
3. The clouds (under the rainbow) covered the mountain.

Suggested appositives are added between commas.

4. My favorite book, *Robinson Crusoe*, lay on the shelf.
5. The boy next door, Sam Miller, climbs our tree.
6. Susan, the lady in the blue dress, is an old friend.

Adjective clauses are in italics.

7. The school *that I attended* has closed.
8. The signed edition of <u>Tom Sawyer</u> *that my parents found* is quite valuable.
9. My brother, *who is well-known for his humor*, tricked me on April Fools' Day.
10. Our trip to England, *which was postponed last year*, is approaching soon.

EXERCISE B: MODIFYING THE PREDICATE

Suggestions for an adverb or adverb phrase for each verb are given below.

1. The stars are shining *brightly*.
2. The car skidded *suddenly*.
3. We climbed the mountain *enthusiastically*.
1. The stars are shining *with intensity*.
2. The car skidded *with a sudden lurch*.
3. We climbed the mountain *with enthusiasm*.

The adverb phrases and clauses are in italics in the sentences below.

4. The garden was planted *in the spring*.
5. We harvested *during the summer*.
6. We took the crops *to market*.
7. *Because an ice storm hit last night*, stores and offices were closed.
8. I cleaned the house *while Mother slept*.
9. *Since I shopped for Christmas early*, I have all my gifts.
10. *When you have finished mowing the lawn*, please trim the hedge.

Exercises C & D

In the sentences below the following are identified: adjective (adj) and adverb (adv) clauses, noun clauses (n), direct (do) and indirect objects (io), predicate nominatives (pn), and predicate adjectives (pa). Each sentence type is also idenfied.

1. The stone *which the builders rejected* (adj) has become the chief *cornerstone* (pn). Cx
2. I will meditate on Your precepts and contemplate Your *ways* (do). S
3. I see wondrous *things* (do) from Your law. S
4. I am a *stranger* (pn) in the earth. S
5. (You) Give *me* (io) *understanding* (do), and I shall keep Your *law* (do). Cd
6. I shall observe *it* (do) with my whole heart. S
7. I hope for Your salvation, and I do Your *commandments* (do). Cd
8. My soul keeps Your *testimonies* (do), and *that I love them exceedingly* (n) is true. Cd-Cx
9. The entirety of Your word is *truth* (pn), and every one of Your righteous judgments endures forever. Cd
10. The Lord will be your *confidence* (pn). S
11. His truth shall be your *shield* and *buckler* (pn). S
12. He is my *refuge* and my *fortress* (pn). S
13. He is our *God*, and we are the *people* of His pasture, and the *sheep* of His hand (pn). Cd
14. The Lord God is a *sun* and a *shield* (pn). S
15. The Lord will give *grace* and *glory* (do) to *whoever cries out to Him* (n). Cx
16. You were once *darkness*, but now you are *light* in the Lord (pn). Cd
17. For we are *members* (pn) of His body. S
18. *That the husband is the head of the wife* (n) is taught in Scripture. Cx
19. *When sin has conceived* (adv), it gives birth to death. Cx
20. *If any of you lacks wisdom* (adv), ask *God* (do). Cx
21. *Blessed* (pa) is the man *who endures temptation* (adj). Cx
22. *When he has been proved* (adv), he will receive the *crown* (do) of life *which the Lord has promised to those who love Him* (adj). Cx
23. *When the chief shepherd appears* (adv), you will receive the *crown* (do) of glory *that does not fade away* (adj). Cx
24. He *who has begun a good work in you* (adj) will complete *it* (do) until the day of Jesus Christ. Cx
25. This is the disciple *who testifies of these things* (adj). Cx
26. His hope is *that you might believe* (n). Cx

Exercise E

8. *My soul keeps Your testimonies, and that I love them exceedingly is true.*

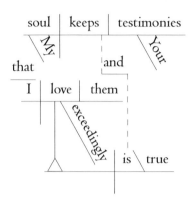

9. *The entirety of Your word is truth, and every one of Your righteous judgments endures forever.*

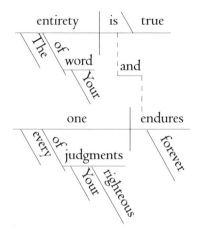

16. *You were once darkness, but now you are light in the Lord.*

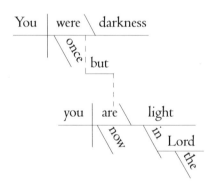

19. *When sin has conceived, it gives birth to death.*

20. *If any of you lacks wisdom, ask God.*

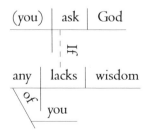

Unit Three: Special Properties of Nouns and Pronouns

Lesson 28: Kinds of Nouns
Exercise
Concrete nouns are listed with a (c), collective with a (col), and abstract with an (a).
retreat (c), duck (c), brood (col), pleasure (a), task (a), shells (c), visitors (c), canals (c), gossip (a), time (a)

Lesson 29: Number
Exercise
1. bushes, roofs, heroes, thieves
2. men, children, oxen, ladies
3. drive-ins, salmon, sheep, glasses
4. ships, sopranos, chiefs, pennies
5. potatoes, sons-in-law, cruises, wives

Lesson 30: Gender
Exercise A
The gender of each of the noun is listed below.
1. Bell (n), uncle (m), strawberry (n), girl (f), neighbor (c), sister (f), tree (n), rose (n), grass (n).
2. Truth (n), goodness (n), clock (n), children (c), grandmother (f), soldier (m), people (c), statesman (m).
3. Stag (m), landlady (f), heir (m), tiger (m), giant (m), countess (f), train (n), brook (n).
4. Son (m), mare (f), lad (m), hero (m), czar (m), client (c), conductor (m), tailor (m), princess (f), book (n).

Lesson 31: Case

Exercise A

1. *Susan* (n) returned the *volleyballs* (o) to the *teacher* (o).
2. The *speaker* (n) delivered the *address* (o) about *femininity* (o) to a large *audience* (o).
3. *Lewis* and *Clark* (n) were famous *explorers* (n) in the *Northwest* (o).
4. This is the finest *restaurant* (n) in the *area* (o).
5. The *horse's* (p) *owner* (n) was worried about the *race* (o).

Exercise B

1. *Susan* (s, f) returned the *volleyballs* (p, n) to the *teacher* (s, c).
2. The *speaker* (s, c) delivered the *address* (s, n) about *femininity* (s, f) to a large *audience* (s, c).
3. *Lewis* (s, m) and *Clark* (s, m) were famous *explorers* (p, c) in the *Northwest* (s, n).
4. This is the finest *restaurant* (s, n) in the *area* (s, n).
5. The *horse's* (s, c) *owner* (s, c) was worried about the *race* (s, n).

Lesson 32: The Declension of a Noun

Exercise A

1. child, children; child, children; child's, children's.
2. beauty, beauties; beauty, beauties; beauty's, beauties'.
3. tongue, tongues; tongue, tongues; tongue's, tongues'.
4. soil, soils; soil, soils; soil's, soils'.
5. family, families; family, families; family's, families'.

Review Exercise

Each italicized noun is followed by the type, number, gender, case, and usage.
1. The oldest *settlement* in our country is *St. Augustine*, Florida.
   settlement: common, singular, neuter, nominative, subject.
   St. Augustine: proper, singular, neuter, nominative, predicate nominative.
2. It was founded by the *Spanish* in 1595.
   Spanish: proper, plural, common, objective, object of the preposition.
3. The *Frenchman* Champlain planted a *colony* in *Canada* about forty *years* later where Quebec now stands.
   Frenchman: proper, singular, masculine, nominative, subject.
   colony: common, singular, neuter, objective, direct object.
   Canada: proper, singular, neuter, objective, object of preposition.

years: common, plural, neuter, objective, object of the preposition.

4. While on an *expedition* in New York *state, Champlain* discovered the *lake* that bears his *name.*

expedition: common, singular, neuter, objective, object of the preposition.

state: common, singular, neuter, objective, object of the preposition

Champlain: proper, singular, masculine, nominative, subject.

lake: common, singular, neuter, objective, direct object

name: common, singular, neuter, objective, direct object

LESSON 33: THE PERSONAL PRONOUN

EXERCISE A

The correct pronouns are in parentheses.

1. She knew it was _____. (I)
2. She and _____ will go together. (he)
3. May Liz and _____ leave now? (I)
4. Mom expects you and _____ for dinner. (me)
5. It was either _____ or her mother who answered the phone. (she)
6. When will you and _____ come again? (they)
7. Have you seen Mark and _____ together? (him)
8. Not many could sing as well as _____. (she)
9. This is the new mind set among _____ Americans. (us)
10. Scott can run faster than _____. (he)

EXERCISE B

The person (1, 2, 3), number (s, p), gender (m, f, c, n), and case (n, o, p) are listed in parentheses.

1. *She* (3, s, f, n) gives much time and money to *her* (3, s, f, p) favorite charities.
2. The boys ran through *their* (3, p, c, p) backyard to *my* (1, s, c, p) house.
3. *He* (3, s, m, n) received a letter from *his* (3, s, m, p) uncle.
4. Mother gave *them* (3, p, c, o) a much deserved lecture in *her* (3, s, f, p) bedroom.
5. *They* (3, p, c, n) will meet *us* (1, p, c, o) at *our* (1, p, c, p) boat dock.
6. *It* (3, s, n, n) is *they* (3, p, c, n) at the door now.
7. If *he* (3, s, m, n) bothers *you* (2, s, c, o) again, let *me* (1, s, c, o) know.
8. Give *him* (3, s, m, o) *my* (1, s, c, p) regards.
9. David and *he* (3, s, m, n) are regulars at the cafe.
10. The winners are Susan and *she* (3, s, f, n).

LESSON 34: WHO, WHOM, WHOSE

EXERCISE A

The correct pronoun is in parentheses.

1. That is the woman (whom) we voted for. Or, That is the woman for (whom) we voted.
2. That is the man (who) responded to my ad.
3. Do you know (who) I am?
4. My father is a person (whom) we all greatly admire.
5. Do you know (whom) the city is named after?
6. Famous American poets were among the writers (whom) we studied.

EXERCISE B

1. *Whom* do you mean?
2. *Whom* have we here?
3. *Whom* will you invite?
4. *Whom* did you give it to?
5. *Who* do you think I am?
6. *Whom* are you writing to?
7. *Whom* were you talking to?
8. *Whom* did she call?
9. I don't know *whom* to send.
10. *Who* was speaking to you?
11. I do not know *whom* he has met.
12. *Who* did you say sat beside you?
13. *Who* do you think will be elected?
14. *Whom* should I meet yesterday but my old friend Jones!
15. *Who* do you think called?
16. *Whom* do you know in your class?
17. You called *whom* at the office?
18. Give the invitations to *whomever* you wish.
19. *Who* is that woman?
20. He is going to be married to *whom*?

Exercise C

The man apologized to the woman whose car he had dented.

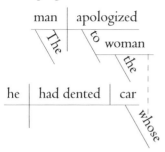

Lesson 35: Other Pronouns

Exercise A

Interrogative (it), demonstrative (d), indefinite (id), or reflexive (r).

1. *Whose* is that? (it)
2. *These* are my mother's pearls. (d)
3. *This* is my old favorite. (d) *Which* is yours? (it)
4. *Who* do you think she is? (it)
5. *What* does that sign say? (it)
6. *Each* said his prayers. (id)
7. She said she would do it *herself*. (r)
8. *Nobody* could agree on a date. (id)
9. *Several* showed up late. (id)
10. *Which* would you like? (it)

Lesson 36: Pronoun Agreement

Exercise A

1. After the concert, all of the students tried to get *their* programs signed by the performers.
2. Either Eric or Mark will be selected to read *his* short story.
3. Everyone in the college is expected to provide *his* own transportation.
4. Every nurse was at *her* station.
5. Each of the boarders has to do *his* own laundry.
6. Several of the instructors brought *their* wives.
7. Every choir member has *his* favorite piece.
8. Nobody in the cab had brought *his* wallet.

9. Katie and her sister were so late *their* father had begun to get worried.

10. Both boys brought *their* luggage with them to the museum.

11. If anyone calls while I am gone, please get *his* number.

12. None of the boys was able to call *his* parents.

13. Few of the preschoolers could tie *their* shoes.

14. Neither runner ran *his* best in the relay.

15. Robert and his brother bought *their* mountain bikes at the yard sale.

16. Everyone demanded *his* opinion be heard.

17. Neither Sue nor Tina ever answered *her* mail.

18. If anyone wants a free ticket, *he* must call today.

19. No one likes to find *himself* uninvited.

20. Neither of the baby birds could lift *its* wings.

21. A young man must make it *his* aim to excel.

22. Few of the dogs are obedient to *their* masters.

23. Some of the people were late to *their* appointments.

24. Emily or Laura will pick up *her* aunt and uncle at the airport.

EXERCISE B

The incorrect pronoun is in italics, followed by the correct pronoun.

1. *their,* his

2. Correct

3. *they,* he

4. Correct

5. *his,* its

6. *themself,* himself

7. *I,* me

8. *his,* their

9. *their,* her

10. *they,* you

UNIT FOUR: SPECIAL PROPERTIES OF VERBS

LESSON 38: THE PRINCIPAL PARTS OF A VERB

EXERCISE A

Infinitive	Present	Past	Present Participle	Past Participle
to be	am/is/are	was	being	(have) been
to drink	drink	drank	drinking	(have) drunk
to come	come	came	coming	(have) come
to go	go/goes	went	going	(have) gone
to swim	swim	swam	swimming	(have) swum
to do	do	did	doing	(have) done
to blink	blink	blinked	blinking	have blinked
to bring	bring	brought	bringing	have brought
to choose	choose	chose	choosing	have chosen
to fly	fly	flew	flying	have flown
to see	see	saw	seeing	have seen
to eat	eat	ate	eating	have eaten
to write	write	wrote	writing	have written
to steal	steal	stole	stealing	have stolen
to throw	throw	threw	throwing	have thrown
to take	take	took	taking	have taken
to fall	fall	fell	falling	have fallen
to give	give	gave	giving	have given
to drive	drive	drove	driving	have driven
to speak	speak	spoke	speaking	have spoken
to pay	pay	paid	paying	have paid
to shrink	shrink	shrank	shrinking	have shrunk
to blow	blow	blew	blowing	have blown
to sink	sink	sank	sinking	have sunk
to know	know	knew	knowing	have known
to ring	ring	rang	ringing	have rung
to draw	draw	drew	drawing	have drawn
to find	find	found	finding	have found
to make	make	made	making	have made
to lay (put)	lay	laid	laying	have laid

to lie (rest)	lie	lay	lying	have lain
to have	have	had	having	have had
to raise	raise	raised	raising	have raised
to rise	rise	rose	rising	have risen

LESSON 40: ACTIVE AND PASSIVE VOICE

EXERCISE A

An *A* marks active; *P* marks passive. The verbs are identified in italics.

1. Eddie *grows* wheat on his farm in the Palouse. *A*
2. His family *has farmed* the same land for three generations. *A*
3. The land *has been plowed* and *planted* many times over the years. *P*
4. Wheat *is planted* in the spring and fall. *P*
5. Some years the farmers *harvest* the crop in early August. *A*
6. Other years the crop *is harvested* in late August. *P*
7. Heavy rains in late summer *can damage* the crop. *A*
8. The crop *can* also *be damaged* by late spring frosts. *P*
9. This year's crop *has* not *been harvested* yet. *P*
10. Passive verbs *can be recognized* easily. *P*

EXERCISE B

The original active sentence is followed by an example of a rewritten passive sentence.

1. I admire her voice. *Her voice is admired by all.*
2. Tulips covered the hillside. *The hillside is covered with tulips.*
3. The wind destroyed my garden. *My garden was destroyed by the wind.*
4. All the family enjoyed the barbecue. *The barbecue was enjoyed by all the family.*
5. I bought a new car last year. *The car was purchased last year.*
6. The skier crossed the wake with ease. *The wake was easily crossed by the skier.*
7. He took a picture of the old bridge. *A picture of the old bridge was taken by him.*
8. The boy mowed the lawn for his neighbor. *The neighbor's lawn was mown by the boy.*
9. The toddler picked the raspberries and ate them. *The raspberries were picked and eaten by the toddler.*
10. The rain left puddles on the sidewalk. *Puddles were left on the sidewalk by the rain.*

EXERCISE C

Conjugation of the verb *to see* in the passive voice.

Principal Parts

Infinitive	Present	Past	Present Participle	Past Participle
to see	see	saw	seeing	(have) seen

Present Tense

Singular	Plural
I am seen	we are seen
you are seen	you are seen
He, she, it is seen	they are seen

Present progressive: I am being seen

Past Tense

Singular	Plural
I was seen	we were seen
you were seen	you were seen
He, she, it was seen	they were seen

Past progressive: I was being seen

Future Tense

Singular	Plural
I shall be seen	we shall be seen
you will be seen	you will be seen
He, she, it will be seen	they will be seen

Future progressive: I shall be being seen

Present Perfect Tense

Singular	Plural
I have been seen	we have been seen
you have been seen	you have been seen
He, she, it has been seen	they have been seen

Present perfect progressive: I have been being seen

Past Perfect Tense (*had* + the past participle)

Singular	Plural
I had been seen	we had been seen
you had been seen	you had been seen
He, she, it had been seen	they had been seen

Past perfect progressive: I had been being seen

Future Perfect Tense (*will have* or *shall have* + past participle)

Singular	Plural
I shall have been seen	we shall have been seen
you will have been seen	you will have been seen
He, she, it will have been seen	they will have been seen

Future perfect progressive: I shall have been being seen

EXERCISE D

1. First person, plural, future, passive of *to praise*: *We shall be praised.*
2. Third person, singular, masculine, past perfect, active of *to sing*: *He had sung.*
3. Second person, plural, present, passive of *to love*: *You are loved.*
4. First person, singular, future perfect, passive of *to fly*: *I shall have been flown.*
5. Third person, plural, past, passive of *to see*: *They were seen.*
6. Third person, singular, feminine, present perfect, passive of *to take*: *She has been taken.*
7. Third person, singular, neuter, past, passive of *to eat*: *It was eaten.*

LESSON 41: MOOD

EXERCISE A

1. In the day of prosperity be joyful, but in the day of adversity consider. (imperative)
2. What profit has he who has labored for the wind? (indicative)
3. Forgive us our trespasses. (imperative)
4. Gather up the fragments that remain. (imperative)
5. I would remain here if you wish. (subjunctive)
6. He might improve, if he would make the effort. (subjunctive)
7. Depart from me, you workers of iniquity. (imperative)
8. Vanity of vanities, all is vanity. (indicative)
9. Better is a poor and wise youth than an old and foolish king who will be admonished no more. (indicative)
10. Fear God and keep His commandments, for this is the whole duty of man. (imperative)

LESSON 42: TRANSITIVE AND INTRANSITIVE VERBS

EXERCISE A

The transitivity of the verbs follows each sentence.
1. Cain *killed* Abel. (transitive)

2. John *wrote* a long letter to his brother. (transitive)

3. God *made* the world. (transitive)

4. She *wept.* (intransitive)

5. The bird *sat* very still on the branch. (intransitive)

6. She *heard* the clock ticking. (transitive)

7. Bill *went* home for summer vacation. (intransitive)

8. Mother *closed* the door. (transitive)

9. The child *loves* his mother. (transitive)

10. The kite *rose* gracefully in the wind. (intransitive)

EXERCISE C

The type of verb is given in parentheses, and its direct object is underlined (if there is one).

1. After the curtain *descended* (intransitive) on the final tableau, Redding *waited* (intransitive) in the lobby while the stream of people *passed.* (intransitive)

2. The Wiggses *had obeyed* (transitive) instructions, and *were* (linking) the very last to come out.

3. They *seemed* (linking) dazed by their recent glimpse into fairy-land.

4. Something in their thin bodies and pinched faces made Redding *form* (transitive) a sudden resolve.

5. "Billy," he said gravely, "can't you and your family *take* (transitive) supper with me?"

6. Billy and his mother *exchanged* (transitive) doubtful glances.

7. For the past three hours everything *had been* (linking) so strange and unusual that they *were* (linking) bewildered.

LESSON 43: AGREEMENT OF SUBJECT AND VERB

EXERCISE A

Select the appropriate verb to agree with the subject in the following sentences.

1. One of the students (is) presenting a paper today.

2. Sally, along with many classmates, (is) signed up for the field trip.

3. Nobody in the class (wants) to miss it.

4. Everyone in the neighborhood (was) at the picnic.

5. Few (were) tardy today.

6. Some of my aunt's dishes (are) broken.

7. Some of my uncle's tobacco (is) missing.

8. (Are) any of you boys going to the gym?

9. (Is) there any reason for this?

10. Law and order (is) the need of the hour.

11. Mr. Jones and Mr. Jacobs (were) absent from the board meeting.

12. (Is) the salt and pepper on the table?

13. Neither hail nor sleet (was) expected.

14. Either the hall or the entryway (is) where I left the letter.

15. Either the dogs or the cat (is) making that noise.

16. The class (is) going skiing this weekend.

17. The cause of the destruction in my garden (is) the bunnies.

18. There (are) my cousins.

19. Six dollars (is) too much to pay.

20. Every car and bus (is) honking (its) horn.

Lesson 44: Review

Review Questions

1. Name the five principal parts of the verb.

   Infinitive, present, past, present participle, past participle

2. What will the infinitive always have in front of it?

   to

3. Which two principal parts will have helping verbs?

   Present participle and past participle

4. What is the difference between a regular and an irregular verb?

   A regular verb forms the past and past participle by adding -ed or -d to the infinitive form. Irregular verbs change their spelling in various ways.

5. What are the principal parts of the verb *to swim*?

   Swim, swim, swam, swimming, have swum

6. Name the six tenses.

   Present, past, future, present perfect, past perfect, future perfect

7. What is unique about the third person singular present tense?

   The verb ends in -s, as in sings.

8. What helping verbs will the future tense always have?

   Will have or shall have

9. What do the perfect tenses have in common?

   The helping verbs have, has, or had

10. The perfect tenses are formed from what principal part?

    Past participle

11. What is the progressive form?

    The -ing form of the verb

12. What does it mean to conjugate a verb?

    To list the verb forms in all tenses, numbers, and persons.

13. Define the active and passive voices.

    When the subject is doing the action it is active voice; when the action is being done to the subject, it is passive voice.

14. Which will always have a helping verb?

    Passive voice

15. Give the first person singular present tense of the active and passive voice of *to call.*

    I call, I am called

16. What is the difference between a transitive and an intransitive verb?

    A transitive verb requires an object to complete the thought; an intransitive does not require an object.

17. Transitive and intransitive verbs are two types of what kind of verb?

    Action verb

18. What are the two other types of verbs?

    Helping verb, linking verb

19. The verb must always agree with its subject in <u>number</u>.

20. What if a prepositional phrase comes between the subject and the verb? Does the verb agree with the subject or the object of the preposition?

    The subject

21. List ten pronouns that are always singular in number.

    I, he, she, it, its, him, her, his, hers, each, either, neither, one, everyone, everybody, no one, nobody, anyone, anybody, someone, somebody.

22. List four pronouns that are always plural in number.

    We, they, them, us

23. Which five pronouns can take either a singular or a plural verb?

    Some, all, any, most, none

24. How do you determine which is required?

    The prepositional phrase that modifies the pronoun determines the number.

25. If the sentence has a compound subject joined by *and*, will the verb be singular or plural?

    Plural

26. Why are some compound subjects joined by *and* (like *peanut butter and jelly*) considered singular?

    We think of them as one thing.

27. Do singular subjects joined by *or* or *nor* take a singular or plural verb?

    Singular

28. What is the rule for a compound subject that includes both a singular and a plural noun?

    The verb agrees in number with the subject nearer to the verb.

29. Explain the rule for collective nouns.

    If the group is considered one unit, it requires a singular verb; if it suggests a collection of individuals acting separately, it is plural.

UNIT 5: VERBALS

LESSON 45: THE PARTICIPLE

EXERCISE A

The participles are in italics below, and the noun each modifies is underlined.

1. We gave him an *illustrated* dinosaur <u>book</u> for his birthday.
2. The *winding* <u>road</u> led to our grandparents' home.
3. She hired a contractor to repair the *damaged* <u>roof</u>.
4. He wanted to grow up to become a *wandering* <u>minstrel</u>.
5. *Migrating* <u>geese</u> fly over our house each fall.
6. The *yelping* <u>puppies</u> tumbled out the door to greet our visitors.
7. The teacher addressed the *assembled* <u>class</u>.
8. My *disappointed* <u>daughter</u> held back her tears.
9. The *exhausted* relay <u>team</u> collapsed in the shade.
10. She looked with curiosity at the *forbidden* <u>box</u>.

EXERCISE B

The participial phrases are in italics in the sentences below.

1. The team, *tired from the heat*, finally won the championship game.
2. *Leading at half-time*, the team had felt confident.
3. The top scorer, *acclaimed for his quickness*, suffered an injury soon after the half.
4. The rest of the team, *wearied from several previous games*, knew they had to work harder.
5. *Plagued by more injuries and poor shots*, the team almost lost.

EXERCISE C

1. *The singing choir marched onto the stage.*

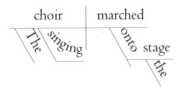

2. *Scaling the wall, the convict nearly escaped.*

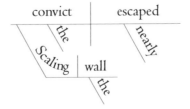

3. *Offering her his hand, he helped her from the car.*

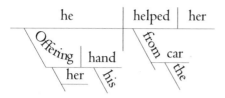

4. *Seeing the large crowd gathered for the occasion, the speaker almost lost his nerve.*

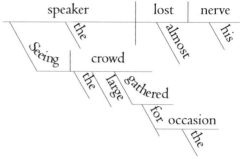

5. *Annoyed at her own clumsiness, the rider got back on the frightened horse.*

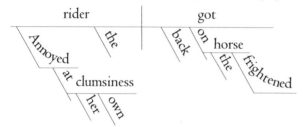

EXERCISE D

	Present Participle	**Past Participle**
1. See	seeing	seen
2. Speak	speaking	spoken
3. Weave	weaving	woven
4. Burn	burning	burnt
5. Grow	growing	grown

EXERCISE E

Examples of rewritten sentences are given below.

1. The huge tree finally gave way to the fierce wind swaying dangerously.

   Swaying dangerously, the huge tree finally gave way to the fierce wind.

2. Spinning his web, the little boy was intrigued by the spider.

   The little boy was intrigued by the spider spinning his web.

3. Rising above the hills, we saw the moon just before midnight.

   We saw the moon rising above the hills just before midnight.

4. We sometimes lose our sense of duty insisting on our rights.

   Insisting on our rights, we sometimes lose our sense of duty.

5. Screaming and chattering, we saw the blue jay in its nest.

We saw the blue jay screaming and chattering in its nest.

Lesson 46: Gerunds

Exercise A

The gerunds in the following sentences are in italics.

1. *Bobbing* for apples is an old-fashioned fall pastime.
2. He won by *running* the last lap full speed.
3. *Swinging* makes her dizzy.
4. The people love the *preaching* at that church.
5. The doctor's chief concern is her erratic *breathing*.

Exercise B

The gerunds and gerund phrases in the following sentences are in italics, and their function in the sentence follows.

1. My mother delights in *baking cookies for her grandchildren.* (object of preposition)
2. *Cleaning the oven* is not my favorite task. (subject)
3. By *printing a retraction,* the error was corrected. (object of preposition)
4. *Forgiving those who wrong you* may be difficult, but it is necessary. (subject)
5. Something that I have always enjoyed is *hanging wallpaper.* (predicate nominative)
6. My vacation last year, *visiting my aunt in Hawaii,* will be hard to top. (appositive)
7. By *gossiping about her friends,* she has created much havoc. (object of preposition)
8. I dislike *playing the accordion.* (direct object)
9. *Listening to the clock chime* is a joy to my grandson. (subject)
10. She loves *surfing and scuba diving in the summer.* (direct object)

Exercise C

1. *He earned money during the summer by mowing lawns.*

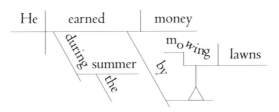

2. *His latest hobby is collecting old coins.*

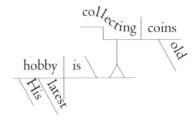

3. *Painting old furniture is her full-time job.*

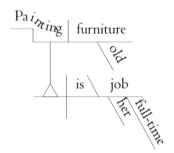

4. *The children love singing in the church choir.*

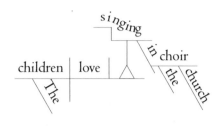

5. *Her assignment, writing several poems, was both difficult and enjoyable.*

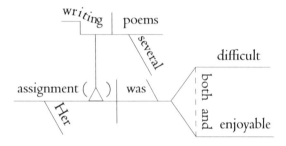

LESSON 47: THE INFINITIVE

EXERCISE A

Each infinitive is in italics followed by how it is used (as noun, adjective, or adverb).

1. This is weather *to watch* (adj.) carefully.

2. I want *to learn* (noun) *to skate* (noun). Note: The first infinitive *to learn* is the direct object of *want* (*want* what? *to learn*). The second infinitive *to skate* is the direct object of the first infinitive *learn* (*learn* what? *to skate*).

3. The young boy tried *to read* (noun) the sign.

4. The plane is ready *to take* (adverb) off.

5. The mechanic *to call* (adjective) is Pete.

6. I want *to tell* (noun) you the truth.

7. Learn *to do* (noun) good.

8. *To obey* (noun) is better than sacrifice.

9. They are in a hurry *to leave* (adjective).

10. That was a day *to remember* (adjective).

EXERCISE B

The infinitives or infinitive phrases in the following sentences are in italics followed by how the infinitive is used (noun, adjective, or adverb). Nouns are followed by how they are used in the sentence.

1. She is a pleasure *to know* (adjective).

2. We are excited *to go on our trip* (adverb). Note: the infinitive phrase modifies the adjective *excited*.

3. This salsa is too hot for me! No infinitive in this sentence.

4. *To succeed*, you must work hard (adverb). Note: the infinitive modifies the adverb *hard*.

5. I like *to spend my vacation time at home* (noun; direct object).

6. She is hoping *to pass her test* (noun; direct object).

7. The boys are ready *to go* (adverb). Note: the infinitive modifies the adjective *ready*.

8. The baby in the tub is so fun *to watch* (adverb). Note: the infinitive modifies the adjective *fun*.

9. *To find the time to exercise* is hard for me (noun; subject).

10. Do you want *to go to the show with me?* (noun; direct object)

EXERCISE C

1. *Take time to do well.*

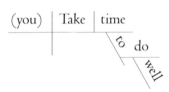

2. *To do well is not easy for the lazy.*

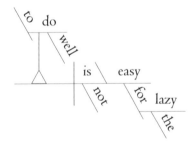

3. *It is hard for them to have a thankless child.*

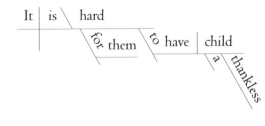

4. *She used to study classics at Oxford before she moved to the States to teach.*

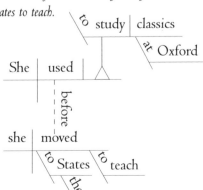

5. *He has the ability to win the race.*

He | has | ability
the / to win | race
the

REVIEW EXERCISE

1. *Racing down the hill, I tried to catch the runaway pony, but he disappeared into the woods before I could reach him.*

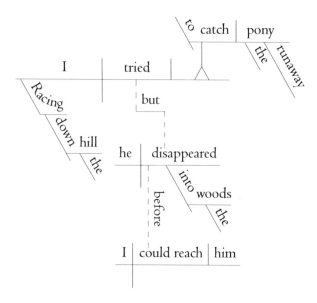

2. *The disappointed crowd is hoping to see the show if the audio can be repaired.*

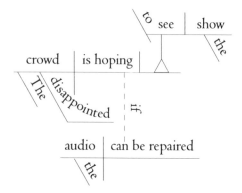

3. *Believing that elves and fairies lived in these hills was once common among the plain folk.*

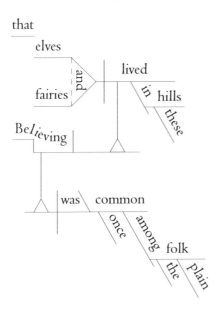

Unit 6: Special Properties of Modifiers

Lesson 48: Comparative and Superlative

Exercise A

The comparative and superlative are listed below. Those that cannot be compared are left blank.

Positive	Comparative	Superlative
good	better	best
rich	richer	richest
virtuous	more virtuous	most virtuous
boiling	———————	———————
destructive	more destructive	most destructive
straight	straighter	straightest
round	rounder	roundest
strong	stronger	strongest
robust	more robust	most robust
sincere	more sincere	most sincere
low	lower	lowest
swift	swifter	swiftest
grateful	more grateful	most grateful
studious	more studious	most studious
little	littler	littlest
extensive	more extensive	most extensive
slowly	more slowly	most slowly
rapid	more rapid	most rapid
soon	sooner	soonest
sweetly	more sweetly	most sweetly
merry	merrier	merriest
brilliant	more brilliant	most brilliant
white	whiter	whitest

Exercise B

The adjectives and adverbs in the sentences are italicized and the degree of comparison of each is listed.

1. Tomorrow promises to be the *most glorious* day. (superlative)
2. The sun is *more brilliant* than the moon. (comparative)

3. That was the *best* rehearsal so far. (superlative)

4. What a *merry little* tune that was. (positive)

5. The shadows are growing *longer*. (comparative)

Exercise C

The sentences are rewritten in italics with corrections. A *C* follows correct sentences.

1. Which of the two books do you like best? *Which of the two books do you like better?*

2. The yard looks more lovelier than it ever has before. *The yard looks lovelier than it ever has before.*

3. I prefer eating at Swilly's than Bonanza. *I prefer eating at Swilly's than eating at Bonanza.*

4. This is the shortest haircut I've ever had. *C*

5. This book is older than all the books in the library. *This book is older than all the other books in the library.*

Lesson 49: Dangling or Misplaced Modifiers

Sample rewritten sentences:

1. She wanted to bake cookies with frosting and sprinkles for the party.

2. While I was practicing the trumpet, the neighbor's dog began howling.

3. When we had driven several blocks, the tailgate flew open.

4. I almost ran over the woman in the large hat with her poodle.

5. While Mom was baking the bread, the house smelled good.